W9-AVI-701

Stephanie Sammartino McPherson

Twenty-First Century Books
Minneapolis

For the courageous children who marched in Birmingham, Alabama, May 1963

The author would like to extend grateful appreciation to Synthia Brown-Dyson for sharing her memories of Coretta Scott King. Thanks also to Sister Cora Marie Billings for discussing her own encounters with Mrs. King. Many thanks also to my editor Anna Cavallo for her insightful suggestions and support.

Twenty-First Century Books
A division of Lerner Publishing Group, Inc.
241 First Avenue North
Minneapolis, MN 55401 U.S.A.

Website addresses: www.lernerbooks.com
www.biography.com

Library of Congress Cataloging-in-Publication Data

McPherson, Stephanie Sammartino.
    Coretta Scott King / by Stephanie Sammartino McPherson.
      p.   cm. — (Biography)
    Includes bibliographical references and index.
    ISBN 978-0-8225-7156-8 (lib. bdg. : alk. paper)
      1. King, Coretta Scott, 1927-2006—Juvenile literature. 2. African American women civil rights workers—Biography—Juvenile literature. 3. Civil rights workers—United States—Biography—Juvenile literature. 4. African Americans—Biography—Juvenile literature. 5. King, Martin Luther, Jr., 1929-1968—Juvenile literature. 6. African Americans—Civil rights—History—20th century—Juvenile literature. 7. Civil rights movements—United States—History—20th century—Juvenile literature. I. Title.
    E185.97.K47M39 2008
    323.092—dc22 [B]   2006039817

Manufactured in the United States of America
1 2 3 4 5 6 – JR – 13 12 11 10 09 08

CONTENTS

In 1983 Coretta Scott King (left) was present when U.S. president Ronald Reagan (seated) signed the legislation that created Martin Luther King Jr. Day.

INTRODUCTION

The White House Rose Garden swarmed with people. Coretta Scott King watched the scene with quiet pride. She had been to the White House before. She had met with presidents, and she had spoken out on important issues. That day, November 2, 1983, she watched as President Ronald Reagan signed a bill important to her and to all Americans. Cameras flashed around her as news reporters vied to capture the historic event.

Thirty pens were lined up before the president. He used them all as he carefully spelled out his name. When he was done, the birthday of Dr. Martin Luther King Jr. had become a national holiday.

Coretta and twenty-nine other privileged observers received the pens as mementoes of the event. Then it was time for Coretta to say a few words. Gazing at the 350 guests, she noted that the United States was a more just and peaceful country because of her husband's work.

Although the ceremony was brief, Coretta had worked for years to bring about this moment. She knew that in honoring her husband's life, she was also continuing his work. Coretta and Martin had struggled and risked great danger to gain freedom and equality for African American citizens. Coretta had marched with Martin. She had sung in freedom concerts to raise money for the civil rights movement. She had also endured threatening phone calls—even the bombing of her home. Still, Coretta refused to give in to fear or to abandon the fight.

Dr. King had traveled frequently to make speeches and organize rallies. Every time he left, Coretta worried about his safety. But she didn't ask him to stay home. If her children had not been so young, she would have been right there beside him at every rally.

Coretta did attend the March on Washington for Jobs and Freedom in August of 1963. She sat behind her husband at the Lincoln Memorial as he spoke words that electrified the entire nation. Martin Luther King Jr. had a dream. He foresaw a time when his four children would be judged not "by the color of their skin but by the content of their character." That dream animated his life.

Less than five years later, Coretta's worst fears were realized. Martin Luther King Jr. was assassinated on April 4, 1968, in Memphis, Tennessee. Even in the midst of her terrible grief, the forty-year-old widow was determined not to let Martin's dream die with him. Within months, she established the Martin Luther King Jr. Memorial Center in Atlanta, Georgia. She held observances at the center on January 15 to commemorate his birthday. Beyond that, she urged people across the nation to remember Martin's life and accomplishments with special ceremonies.

For more than a decade, Coretta lobbied and campaigned to have her husband's birthday declared a national holiday. She testified before Congress and initiated petition drives. By 1982 the King Center had collected more than six million signatures on petitions calling for the holiday. Coretta and singer Stevie Wonder took them to the Speaker of the House of Representatives, Tip O'Neil.

Legislators could not ignore the tremendous popular support. The next year, both houses of Congress voted in favor of a federal holiday to honor Martin Luther King Jr. Coretta was overjoyed. It was a time for celebration, a time for remembering a courageous and dedicated leader. But it was also a time to look forward. Later Coretta would explain that Martin Luther King Jr. Day was not just for African Americans but for everyone. Her husband's dream had encompassed people of all races, religions, and ethnic groups. She looked to the nation's young people to fulfill Martin's vision of justice, freedom, and equality for all Americans.

As a child, Coretta—like some other African American children of the 1930s (above)—worked in the cotton fields to help support their families.

Chapter **ONE**

DETERMINED TO SUCCEED

NOBODY HAD TO TELL CORETTA SCOTT THAT THE world was unfair. Even as a small child, she figured that out on her own. She was born near Marion, Alabama, on April 27, 1927. At the time, there was little justice for African Americans in the South. All the best jobs went to white people, and blacks were denied many basic rights. Strict regulations, known as Jim Crow laws, aimed to keep the races rigidly separated in society. On buses and in restaurants, African Americans were treated as second-class citizens. They couldn't even drink from the same water fountains as white people. And black children were forced to attend different schools from white children.

When Coretta was a child, the school buildings that states provided for African American students were often old and small. Black schools usually got cast-off furniture from schools for white children.

The state provided educational facilities that were supposedly separate but equal. Coretta had never seen the inside of the white grade school, but she knew instinctively that her own school could not compare with it. At Coretta's school, first through sixth graders were crowded together in a single room. Books were in very short supply. There were no indoor bathrooms, and the only heat came from a wood-burning stove. In addition, the school district did not provide a bus for black children. Each day, the bus transporting white children whizzed by Coretta as she walked three miles from her family's farm to school. The unequal treatment made her angry.

As Good As Everyone Else

Obadiah and Bernice Scott, Coretta's parents, would have done anything for their children. But they couldn't make life fair for Coretta. Everywhere she went outside of the African American community, Coretta faced bigotry (harsh intolerance). In the movie theater, she and her black friends would climb the stairs to the balcony. It was harder to see from up there. But the seats below were all reserved for white children.

After school, if Coretta wanted to buy an ice cream cone at the drug store, the white owner did not allow her into the building. Instead he made all the African American children wait outside a side door while he served other customers. Only after all the white children had their ice cream did he get around to helping the black children. Then he served the black youngsters whatever flavor he wanted to get rid of.

Coretta, her older sister, Edythe, and her younger brother, Obadiah (nicknamed Obie), were used to such treatment. But they knew it was wrong. Did things have to be this way? Puzzled and hurt, Coretta went to her mother. She wondered, why couldn't she sit inside the drugstore? Or go to a modern school with plenty of books? Why couldn't she play in the same parks with white children or sit wherever she wanted on the bus?

Bernice Scott ached with grief for her child's distress. She could only reply that Coretta was just as good as everyone else. There was no justification for the unfair situations she faced.

Coretta was a lively, outgoing child who enjoyed visiting her grandparents nearby and romping through the fields with boys. Sometimes, though, her temper surfaced. When displeased, Coretta resorted to throwing sticks and small pebbles at her companions. Years later she recalled fighting a lot.

But music could soothe Coretta's woes. She listened to all kinds of recordings on the family's Victrola record player. She also loved to sing. When Coretta sang, she felt confident and happy.

Despite the prejudice they faced daily, Coretta's parents taught their children not to judge others on the basis of race. Obadiah Scott maintained that some white people were good. Bernice Scott believed that the key to a better life lay in education. She had been forced to stop school after fourth grade, but she was determined to see her children go to college. She urged them to get an education so they could be successful in life. Then they wouldn't have to depend on anyone else.

HARD WORKERS

Coretta was only about six or seven, scarcely big enough to lift a hoe, when she started working in her family's garden. Obadiah Scott depended on his children's help on the farm, because he had another job transporting lumber for a nearby sawmill. He used his own truck to haul the logs and timber from the forest. The only other people in the area who owned trucks were white. Some of them felt threatened by Obadiah's success. Often Obadiah's job took him deep into the woods to pick up logs. Encountering him on a deserted stretch of road, resentful whites would force his truck to a standstill. Then they swore at him and threatened his life. Often Coretta heard her father tell her mother that he might not get back from one of his jobs hauling timber. Coretta felt a pang of apprehension every time he left in his truck. The incident was repeated over and over, but she never got used to it.

Money was tight for everyone during the 1930s, a period known as the Great Depression. When Coretta was ten years old, she took a job on a neighboring cotton farm owned by a white man. The money she earned helped pay for her school supplies. Coretta worked hard and fast. When it was time to pick the fluffy cotton bolls, she easily outstripped her boy cousins in the amount of cotton she picked.

A GIFT FOR MUSIC

Church played an important role in Coretta's life. Every Sunday Coretta attended the African Methodist Episcopal church. The minister made sure his congregation knew that God loves everyone. If an incident of racial violence had occurred recently, the minister told the people to keep on praying and that God would take care of things. Coretta never forgot his words, and she never stopped praying. During the service, both of Coretta's grandfathers led the congregation in song. Following their example, Coretta sang the hymns with deep feeling.

In 1939, when Coretta finished sixth grade, she went to Lincoln High School, 10 miles (16 kilometers) away. All the students were African American, but some of the teachers were white. For this reason, Lincoln was considered a semiprivate school. Since there was no bus, and 10 miles was too far to walk, Coretta boarded with an African American family in the town of Marion. Walking to and from the school, Coretta and her friends became the targets of vicious taunting. White students coming down the sidewalk would band together and try to push the black students out of the way, insulting them with racial slurs. Sometimes Coretta was scared, but she refused to abandon the sidewalk.

Lincoln High School was worth the difficulty of getting there. Coretta's musical talent blossomed under an excellent teacher. She learned to read music and to play the flutophone (similar to a recorder) and the trumpet. She took voice lessons and won solo parts in school music productions. Later she became the pianist and the choir director at her church. Coretta began to think that she wanted to dedicate her life to music.

FAMILY STRUGGLES

Harsh reality kept intruding on Coretta's dreams. Her family's home went up in flames on Thanksgiving evening of 1942. The Scotts had excitedly moved into the six-room house several years earlier. Coretta and Edythe had enjoyed the luxury of having a bedroom of their own. The cause of the fire was never determined. Investigators said that since the house lay outside the city limits, there was little they could do. But Coretta suspected the fact that the family was black had something to do with the authorities' lack of interest in the matter.

The Scotts were not a family to give in to misfortune. They rolled up their sleeves and continued to work. Eager to help his children, Obadiah turned a truck he owned into a school bus. Coretta's mother became the driver, taking students back and forth to Lincoln High School each day. Thanks to her parents' determination, Coretta could live at home again.

And thanks to his years of hard work hauling timber, Obadiah Scott was finally able to buy his own sawmill. But some white workers were upset to see an African American prosper. A white logger who worked for him wanted to own the mill himself. When Obadiah refused to sell, the logger uttered a veiled threat. He said that Obadiah's endeavor would not succeed. Within days the sawmill had burned to the ground.

Obadiah felt there was little use in going to the law. He simply went on with his life the best he could. His moral courage inspired Coretta not to give in to hatred either.

At that time, not many women of any race went to college. But Coretta wanted a better life than she knew she could have in the South. In 1945, while in twelfth grade, she applied to Antioch College, an integrated institution in Yellow Springs, Ohio. Her sister, Edythe, was already a student at Antioch and encouraged her to attend. Coretta was thrilled when she received a partial scholarship. She was getting the education her mother always wanted her to have. And she was going north!

Coretta started school at Antioch College in Yellow Springs, Ohio, in 1945.

Chapter **TWO**

BIG DREAMS

CORETTA JOINED A FRESHMAN CLASS IN WHICH THERE were only two other black students. Many people expected the African American male in Coretta's class to escort her to dances and campus events. Coretta had nothing against the young man, but she would not go out with him. She wanted to have more in common with a date than just their race. Later she dated a white student who shared her love of music.

FIGHTING SEGREGATION IN THE NORTH

As much as she yearned to perform, Coretta knew she had to be practical in her career choice. Teaching music seemed a good way to combine her passion with a steady income. Coretta enrolled in Antioch's education program, where she was required to do two years of practice teaching. At first, Coretta worked in the private elementary school that was run by the college. For the second year, she was supposed to teach in one of the city's public schools. Since African American children attended the Yellow Springs public schools side by side with white children, Coretta did not anticipate a problem. She was shocked when the school board turned down her application to teach. Although the student body was integrated, the teachers were all white.

Indignantly Coretta complained to the college president, but he refused to champion her cause. He said she could continue to teach in Antioch's private school, or she could go to the nearby town of Xenia. In Xenia, African American and white students attended separate schools. Coretta was deeply frustrated. She could not muster support among the faculty or her fellow students. But she refused to go to Xenia. She had left Alabama to get away from segregation.

To receive her degree, Coretta had to finish her practice teaching at the school run by the college. Still she was determined to do something positive with her anger. Coretta became active in Antioch's branch of the National Association for the Advancement of Colored People (NAACP). She also joined the Civil Liberties Committee and the Race Relations Committee. Change would take a long time, she realized, but at least she was making a start.

BIG DREAMS

Coretta's study of music proved happier than her practice teaching. Impressed with her vocal talent, her teachers encouraged her to perform. Coretta gave her first public concert in 1948 in Springfield, Ohio. The audience applauded enthusiastically.

Soon more concert opportunities came Coretta's way. Paul Robeson, a famous African American singer, came to Antioch College to sing at an NAACP event. Coretta was asked to perform on the same program. She must have been nervous, but she did what she always did. She went onstage and lost herself in the music. Paul Robeson was delighted with the quality of her voice. He urged her to get all the vocal training she could.

Coretta took his encouragement to heart. As graduation approached in 1951, she applied to the best music schools in the country. Instead of teaching, she might become an opera singer after all. Finally she decided to attend the New England Conservatory of Music in Boston, Massachusetts. All she had to do was find the money for tuition.

Coretta's father was successful enough to pay her expenses and willing to help out. When she visited home, however, Coretta decided not to ask him for help. At twenty-four years old, she felt it was time she met her own financial needs. Concerned but optimistic, Coretta boarded the train to Boston. Somehow, she knew, she would find a way to pay her tuition.

Coretta probably wasn't thinking about money when she called her parents from New York City. But they had exciting news. Coretta had received a letter from the Jesse Smith Noyes Foundation, offering her a grant of $650 to pursue her musical training. Relief swept over Coretta. She could relax and enjoy the final portion of her journey to Boston.

Despite her grant, Coretta had a difficult time making ends meet. The grant covered her tuition but not her living expenses. When Coretta's money ran low, she ate graham crackers, peanut butter, and fruit for dinner. Two nights in a row, she didn't have any dinner at all. In desperation, she struck a deal with her landlady. She did cleaning in exchange for her room and free breakfasts. She also took a part-time job with a mail-order company. It was a hectic schedule, but Coretta was strong and ambitious. She was doing what she loved best—taking voice lessons and studying music. She had big dreams for her future.

A GIFTED YOUNG MINISTER

Coretta had been in Boston about six months when she received a phone call from a young African American minister. His name was Martin Luther King Jr., and he was working on his doctorate degree in theology. He explained that a mutual friend, Mary Powell, had given him Coretta's phone number. Mary had been so enthusiastic about Coretta that Martin was eager to meet her.

Coretta remembered Mary saying nice things about

Martin too. Soon Martin and Coretta were chatting away on the phone as if they were old friends. Coretta enjoyed his lively manner. While they were talking, Martin compared himself to Napoleon at the Battle of Waterloo. In that battle, Napoleon had finally been defeated. Martin implied that he too had been conquered—by Coretta's graciousness and all the good things he had heard about her. They decided to meet for lunch the next day.

When Martin picked up Coretta at the music conservatory, she felt a twinge of disappointment. He was much shorter than she had imagined. Then she became

Coretta met Martin in Boston. He was a theology student at Boston College.

fascinated by his thoughtful conversation. As Coretta listened, Martin seemed to grow taller in her eyes. She couldn't help but like and respect him.

Driving Coretta back to school that day, Martin mentioned that she had all the qualities he hoped to find in his future wife. Coretta was startled. How could Martin know that after only one meeting? she protested.

But Martin felt he had already discovered everything he needed to know. He told Coretta that she had "character, intelligence, personality, and beauty." What more could he possibly want?

Coretta was flattered, flustered, and hesitant. She had enjoyed Martin's company greatly. But she had to finish school and launch her career. The last thing she wanted to think about was marriage.

THE POWER OF LOVE

Early in their relationship, Martin told Coretta of his deep admiration for Mohandas Gandhi. Preaching love as a powerful weapon against injustice, Gandhi had advocated nonviolent resistance to British rule in India. His courage and goodness influenced countless people and helped bring about the independence of his country. Martin called Gandhi the first person since the beginning of Christianity to expand Jesus's teachings about love into a means to achieve social change.

DETERMINED SUITOR

Coretta did her best to withstand Martin's charm. But a part of her must have known all along that it wasn't any use. Martin was brilliant, gallant, and concerned with the well-being of African Americans. One Sunday Martin took her to hear him preach at a nearby Baptist church. Coretta found herself deeply caught up in Martin's stirring words. She was touched when Martin asked her to a concert at Boston's Symphony Hall. It meant a great deal to her that Martin wanted to share her love of music.

But Martin wasn't above a bit of mischief. Sometimes he pretended to like other girls. Coretta would respond with indignation—until she noticed Martin laughing at her. He thought it was a great joke to make her jealous.

Coretta loved Martin's dedication, sensitivity, and humor. But what would happen to her career if she married him? Coretta longed to perform onstage. Yet she also yearned for a husband and children. She struggled with feeling pulled in two directions.

That summer Coretta visited Martin's family in Atlanta, Georgia. Once again she heard Martin preach, this time at Ebenezer Baptist Church. His father was pastor of the church, so Martin knew the congregation well. Coretta watched him reach out to church members with kindness and warmth. Her heart was full of pride in the boyfriend she was thinking of marrying. But she was disappointed that his parents did not seem to take her relationship with Martin seriously.

Coretta met Martin's parents again when they came to see their son in Boston that November. Soon she realized they were not pleased with her daily visits to Martin's apartment. Martin Luther King Sr., known as Daddy King, told Coretta about the lovely girls his son had dated in Atlanta.

When Daddy King mentioned the fine qualities these girls would bring to a marriage with Martin, Coretta was stung. She retorted that she had a great deal to offer Martin too. She wished that Martin would stand up for her. But Martin simply left the room. Later he told Coretta that he had gone to speak to his mother. Martin had informed her that he planned to marry Coretta.

Mrs. King must surely have repeated those words to her husband. However much Daddy King hoped for Martin to marry an Atlanta girl, he knew his son loved Coretta dearly. And she certainly had spunk. Putting aside his reservations, he consented to the marriage.

By this time, Coretta knew that her life would never be complete without Martin. On June 18, 1953, Coretta and Martin were married on the lawn of her parents' house. A nervous bride, Coretta had originally hoped to keep the guest list small. But the wedding grew into the largest one the town had ever seen. Daddy King performed the ceremony. At Coretta's request, he removed the word "obey" from the marriage vows. Both the groom and his father understood Coretta well enough to know that she had a mind of her own. She was not about to blindly obey anyone.

HAPPY YOUNG COUPLE

When the newlyweds left the reception, Coretta drove so that an exhausted Martin could grab a quick nap. Since no hotels nearby allowed African Americans, the couple spent that night at a friend's house. The friend worked as an undertaker, and Martin later liked to joke about spending their wedding night in a funeral home.

Martin and Coretta deeply enjoyed each other's company.

Within days of their wedding, Coretta joined the Baptist Church so she could fully share Martin's religion. Wearing a white robe for her baptism, Coretta walked into the waist-high pool behind the choir loft. Daddy King, in a black robe over a rubber suit, ducked her head under water as part of the ritual.

That summer the new Reverend and Mrs. King lived with Martin's parents in their large home. Coretta worked as a bank clerk until it was time for her to return to Boston with Martin. Both were determined to complete their education.

Coretta plunged eagerly into her studies. It was demanding but joyful work. Coretta took piano and voice lessons, and she had classes in choir directing and musical arrangements for orchestra. She studied string instruments as well as woodwinds, brass, and percussion. The hard work paid off. Coretta was excited to receive a role in the opening performance of a work by a well-respected Cuban composer. This was a great honor, but it also meant many hours of rehearsal. Martin cooked on Thursday nights and pitched in with the housework.

As she had at Antioch, Coretta was required to do practice teaching at the Boston Conservatory. Her duties took her to three schools where she was the only African American teacher. Much to her relief, the children liked her and readily took part in musical events. Coretta enjoyed the whole experience.

As the academic year wound down, the Kings had to

consider their future. Martin had completed all the coursework for his doctorate. It was time to look for his first job as a minister. Coretta hoped he would find a nice church in the North. She didn't want to give up the freedom they enjoyed in Boston. She also felt the North offered more opportunities for an aspiring singer.

Martin had different ideas. He wanted to go south precisely because of the hardships African Americans there faced. Coretta and Martin talked and prayed about the decision. When Martin elected to take a position at the Dexter Avenue Baptist Church in Montgomery, Alabama, Coretta did her best to talk him out of it. But Martin remained firm.

Despite her strong misgivings about Alabama, Coretta found that she liked Dexter Church. The first time she visited the church, Martin introduced her to the congregation and asked her to speak a few words. The worshipers responded enthusiastically to Coretta's quiet dignity and warmth. Coretta was touched. As she might have suspected, the minister's residence, where she and Martin would live, was located in a segregated neighborhood and needed a great deal of fixing up. But as Coretta wandered through the rooms, she decided she could turn it into a real home. More important, she believed she would fit in with the congregation. She told Martin she would support him in every way. If he wanted to be a pastor in Montgomery, she would make herself happy there.

Coretta and Martin enjoyed their new life together in
Montgomery, Alabama.

Chapter **THREE**

THE MONTGOMERY BUS BOYCOTT

CORETTA AND MARTIN SOON SETTLED INTO THEIR comfortable new life. As the pastor's wife, Coretta was always busy. She served as Martin's secretary, worked on committees, and sang in the church choir. She wanted it to become the finest choir in all of Montgomery. In addition to her own activities, Coretta took a keen interest in everything Martin was doing. He belonged to the NAACP and to the local branch of the Alabama Council on Human Relations. Like him, Coretta cared passionately about social justice.

In the spring of 1955, Coretta learned that she was pregnant. As she happily prepared for her new baby, she thought about where she wanted to give birth to her child. Only one hospital in Montgomery, the City of St. Jude Catholic Hospital, allowed African Americans and whites to share the same wards. Coretta felt she would be treated with respect and competence there. On November 17, 1955, her daughter Yolanda Denise was born. Coretta was filled with happiness. She loved to watch Martin cuddle the baby when he came home from work.

TIME FOR ACTION

Baby Yolanda (nicknamed Yoki) was less than three weeks old when her father received an early morning call. Martin shared his distressing phone conversation with Coretta. The previous evening, December 1, a forty-two-year-old seamstress named Rosa Parks had been riding the bus home. Montgomery buses were strictly segregated, and Parks had been in the first row of seats available to black patrons. All of the seats for white people were already occupied when more whites boarded the bus. The driver demanded that Parks give up her seat, following the local custom.

Rosa Parks was tired of complying with such unfair customs. She did not relish standing up for the rest of the ride. Calmly she looked at the bus driver and replied, "No." He promptly called the police. Parks was arrested and charged with breaking the city's segregation laws, even though she had been sitting in the black section of the bus.

Word of Parks's arrest had spread quickly overnight. The African American community sizzled with anger.

After Rosa Parks's arrest for refusing to give up her seat on a city bus, a police officer takes her fingerprints.

Black citizens resented the indignities they faced daily, and they were ready to take action. E. D. Nixon, the man who called Dr. King with the news, had served as president of the local branch of the NAACP. He felt there was only one way to signal to whites the frustration and anger that African Americans were feeling. They should boycott (stop riding) the buses as a form of protest.

Martin agreed wholeheartedly. He was so supportive of the idea that he offered his church as a meeting place to discuss the issue. Coretta couldn't attend the meeting because she had to care for the baby, but Martin told her all about it. The boycott was scheduled to begin three days later on the date of Parks's trial, December 5. "Don't ride the buses to work, to town, to school, or anywhere on Monday," urged the boycott organizers. They would hold another meeting Monday evening. Then they would determine if the protest should go on longer.

Coretta soon found herself busier than ever. When she wasn't feeding the baby, she was answering the phone or helping to arrange alternate transportation for African Americans. The people who usually rode the buses would need some other way to get to work.

The night before the boycott, Martin and Coretta stayed up late talking. Both were worried. This was not the first boycott African Americans had staged in the South. Earlier efforts had not proved successful, but Martin and Coretta clung to hope. They agreed that if only 60 percent of the usual patrons avoided the buses, the boycott would have made a powerful statement.

By 5:30 the next morning, Coretta and Martin were up again. A bus stop was just outside their house. At 6:00 A.M., the first bus was scheduled to stop. Coretta stationed herself at the front window, tense with anticipation. Suddenly her heart pounded. Excitedly she called for Martin. The bus had arrived. Rows and rows of empty seats showed in the brightly lit interior. Not a single passenger was inside. Usually the bus was jammed with people. Giddy with excitement, Coretta and Martin waited for the next bus. It too was empty. The boycott was off to a fantastic start!

A MOVEMENT IS BORN

All over the city it was the same thing—empty buses. African Americans walked to work or took taxis. Some hitched horses to buggies or rode mules. People were willing to walk 12 miles (19 km) rather than set foot in a bus. That afternoon a leaders' meeting was called. A new organization called the Montgomery Improvement Association (MIA) was formed to keep the boycott running. It would eventually become an important group within the civil rights movement. Martin was unanimously elected president. Coretta realized that he would spend many hours away from his family and be in considerable danger as the most obvious target of white people's anger. But she was willing to accept hardship and risk for the cause. Whatever her husband had to do, she promised her complete support.

Martin spoke at the public meeting that evening. He'd had only twenty minutes to compose one of the most crucial speeches of his career. But in a way, Martin had

Martin's speech rallied members of Montgomery's African American community to stay off city buses.

been preparing for this speech all his life. As a people, African Americans had been incredibly patient, he declared. But patience wasn't a virtue when it meant accepting injustice. It was time for African Americans to claim their full rights as citizens. A white newspaper reporter called the meeting "the beginning of a flame that would go across America." The audience voted unanimously to continue the boycott. They would not support the bus company until it agreed to hire black drivers, treat black passengers more courteously, and cease the practice of ordering them to give up their seats for whites.

Day after day, African Americans avoided the buses. The bus company was losing money. Many white people were stunned and angered by the spirit and determination with which African Americans continued the boycott. They vented a great deal of anger on the Kings. Coretta knew that a vengeful act of violence could take everything she had in an instant. She steeled herself to the insults, abuse, and threats she sometimes received when she answered the phone. One caller said that that the Kings would be killed if they didn't leave town. Another said they would be sorry they ever came to Alabama.

Coretta and Martin did not respond with anger. Instead they preached nonviolence in all circumstances. By this they did not mean that African Americans should remain passive. They were to be forceful, even militant, in their demands for justice. But they were never to give in to hatred. Martin believed it took more courage to endure aggression than to retaliate. Such courage and faith would ultimately change the hearts and minds of those who were bigoted. Martin's message to those who re- sisted integration was simple. African Americans would not hate anyone, but they would not obey unjust laws. In the end, their moral strength would overcome the physical strength of those who opposed them.

However frightened Coretta may have been inside, she kept up a strong demeanor. And despite the abusive calls, Coretta kept answering the phone. Someone coor- dinating the boycott or arranging carpools might be calling.

Running her household was also a challenge. Coretta never knew how many extra people Martin might bring home to dinner. Other times urgent business kept Martin from arriving home on time. Coretta waited while the food she had prepared grew cold. But she never com- plained. What Martin was doing was more important than supper.

Less than two years earlier, Coretta had not wanted to live in the South. But she was glad to be someplace where she could help Martin make a positive impact on the lives of African Americans. By the end of January, Coretta and Martin were sure that the growing civil rights movement would spread beyond Montgomery. They hoped that it would have national repercussions.

The strength of the new movement was evident when Martin was arrested for allegedly driving 5 miles (8 km) over the speed limit. So many people hastened to the jail where Martin was being detained that the police were alarmed. Finally, the jailer let Martin go. But some whites were angered by Martin's release. Several days later, the Kings received more than thirty hate calls. Weary and angry, Coretta took the phone off the hook at 2:30 A.M. It was the only way to get a few hours of sleep.

MEETING VIOLENCE WITH NONVIOLENCE

As the threatening phone calls increased, Martin became more concerned about Coretta and Yoki. He hated to leave them at night. Coretta assured Martin that she had no fears about staying alone. But she did let Martin arrange for a companion to stay with her one night in 1956 when he had to address a large gathering. As Coretta and her friend, Mary Lucy Williams, were chatting that night, something heavy thumped on the front porch. Instantly the two women were hurrying toward the back of the house for safety. There was a deafening explosion and a burst of shattering glass. Smoke began to fill the rooms. Mary Lucy screamed, heightening Coretta's own panic.

Groping her way to the baby's room, Coretta found Yolanda safe. For the moment, that was all that mattered. As she soothed her daughter, Coretta automatically reached for the telephone. Then she stopped short. Whom could she call? She knew the police would be no help. Many police officers thought the Kings were troublemakers who had to be stopped.

News of what happened traveled quickly. By the time a frantic Martin arrived, a large crowd had gathered around the house. People were angry. Many carried guns; others held rocks or bottles. They were ready to exact revenge for the attack on their respected leader. The police could scarcely maintain order. Silently Coretta prayed for the safety of her family and for peace.

Martin addressed the rebellious mob, urging them not to resort to violence. They should treat their enemies with kindness. They should love all people, even the ones who had bombed the Kings' home.

Martin's words had a calming effect on the crowd. Many were inspired to lay aside their anger and confront violence with forgiveness. As the people began to disperse, Coretta noted that some had tears in their eyes.

The Kings spent the rest of the night at the home of friends. Soon Daddy King arrived from Atlanta. Coretta's father also came when he heard the news. He wanted to take his daughter and grandchild home with him until everything clamed down.

Coretta was frightened about what the angry white bigots might do next. She desperately wanted to protect her baby. But she could not back down from what she had helped Martin begin. Despite the pleas of both fathers, Coretta and Martin decided to stay in Montgomery. They felt they had to continue the fight that they believed in so strongly.

Coretta greets Martin with a kiss as he leaves court in Montgomery, Alabama, on March 22, 1956.

Chapter **FOUR**

NATIONAL SPOTLIGHT

THE CITY OF MONTGOMERY WOULD GO TO ANY lengths to stop the bus boycott. Searching through old ordinances, officials discovered a regulation against boycotts. In March 1956, a court found Martin guilty of breaking this long-forgotten law. Martin was released on bail. When he and Coretta left the courtroom, they found hundreds of people waiting for them. Instead of accepting defeat, they sang, "We ain't gonna ride the buses no more."

Martin's lawyers did not plan to accept defeat either. They appealed the conviction with a lawsuit of their own. They petitioned to have bus segregation in Montgomery, Alabama, declared unconstitutional.

A Federal District Court agreed with the lawyers' arguments. Two months after Martin's initial arrest, the court decreed that bus segregation did indeed violate the Constitution. But it was too soon to celebrate victory. The city appealed the decision to the U.S. Supreme Court. Nothing would change until the Supreme Court ruled.

On October 30, the city also started proceedings to have carpools declared illegal. Officials claimed that the voluntary carpools were really a business that was operating without a license. This was a serious threat to the boycott. For nearly a year, many African Americans had relied on carpools to get to work. If carpooling came to a halt, they would be forced back onto the buses. The boycott would fail.

Coretta and Martin had little confidence that their own attorneys would prevail. Was this the end of the boycott that had started out with such promise and determination? Sitting in the courtroom on November 13, Coretta thought that it was just a matter of time until the judge outlawed carpools.

Around noon there was a slight disturbance in the courtroom. Reporters began milling around in agitation. One newsman handed Martin a sheet of paper. Coretta, seated farther back in the room, could see that her husband and the other people at the defendants' table were becoming excited. Martin sprang from his chair and hurried to Coretta's side. Joyfully he announced that the U.S. Supreme Court had declared Alabama's bus segregation laws unconstitutional.

The stunning news rippled across the courtroom. The emerging civil rights movement had won a major victory.

For bigoted whites, however, the defeat was bitter. An angry backlash struck the city that night. The Kings received more threatening phone calls. The Ku Klux Klan, a racist organization, drove through town and attempted to frighten African Americans. But the black citizens of Montgomery refused to be intimidated. They had too much to celebrate.

SINGING FOR FREEDOM

As the citizens of Montgomery waited for the Supreme Court order to reach city officials, Coretta kept busy rehearsing music and writing a script. The first anniversary of the boycott was approaching. To commemorate this milestone, some civil rights activists had organized a large concert in New York. The proceeds from concert ticket sales would go to the Montgomery Improvement Association. Coretta was to take the leading role in the program, performing with such music legends as Duke Ellington and Harry Belafonte.

On December 5, 1956, a very nervous Coretta walked onstage before a sold-out auditorium. Despite her stage fright, she had a powerful presence and quiet integrity that captivated her audience. Coretta began by singing classical numbers. Then she told the story of the bus boycott in narrative and song. At last Coretta had found a way to share her love of music and to help the civil rights movement at the same time.

JUST THE BEGINNING

About two weeks after the concert, Coretta waved good-bye to Martin and watched him walk from their door to the bus stop. When the bus arrived, Martin chose a front seat, which he shared with a white minister, Glenn Smiley. From then on, African Americans could sit anywhere they chose on Montgomery city buses.

Coretta and Martin were thrilled with their accomplishments, but they knew this was just the beginning. Prejudice and bigotry still existed all over the South, and in the North as well. It was time to extend the civil rights movement beyond Montgomery. Martin decided to hold a conference in January 1957, in his hometown of Atlanta, to discuss the next step. Coretta helped her husband prioritize the issues to be discussed at the meeting. Full of anticipation, she accompanied Martin to Atlanta.

The night before the conference, however, Martin received word of more violence in Montgomery. Angry whites had bombed the home and the church of Martin's good friend Reverend Ralph Abernathy. Other bombs exploded in the city. Martin and Reverend Abernathy hurried back to Montgomery to defuse the situation. They could not allow the hatred and destruction to escalate. Coretta took her husband's place at the conference, explaining what had happened in Montgomery and submitting an agenda for consideration. A temporary organization was formed, and another conference was scheduled for February in New Orleans.

The Kings were still in grave danger. Before the second

After the end of the boycott, Coretta (front, fourth from left) *and Martin* (third from left) *wait together at a Montgomery bus stop.*

meeting, a pile of dynamite sticks was left on the Kings' front porch. Luckily, someone spotted the dynamite before it could explode. Despite the threat, Martin held fast to his nonviolent approach and urged people not to retaliate. But he also knew that African Americans must not give up the struggle for equality. On February 14, 1957, the new Southern Christian Leadership Conference (SCLC)—a group that would support and encourage nonviolent protests for civil rights—elected Martin as its president.

FREEDOM IN GHANA

The national and international publicity that the civil rights movement received turned Martin into a celebrity. His fame extended to Africa, where President Kwame Nkrumah, the new president of Ghana, invited the Kings to a momentous event. A British colony for many years,

Ghana was about to become a free nation. Coretta and Martin attended the Independence Day ceremonies in the capital city of Accra. On March 6, 1957, they saw 50,000 citizens of Ghana, some of them wearing their colorful traditional clothing, crammed into the town square. "Ghana is free!" citizens exclaimed joyfully. Coretta never forgot the exhilaration of that moment.

JOYS AND FEARS

The King family continued to grow. Coretta and Martin welcomed a baby boy into their lives on October 23, 1957. The happy parents named him Martin Luther King III. Two-year-old Yoki and newborn Marty were the joy of Coretta's life. She cherished the times when her entire family was together. But she understood why her husband had to travel so much. He needed to gain nationwide support for the civil rights movement.

One evening, Coretta, visiting Martin's family in Atlanta, was quietly anticipating his return from a trip when the phone rang. A family friend told her to prepare herself for bad news. Martin had been stabbed by a mentally deranged African American woman in Harlem, New York. Immediately Coretta left to be with him.

Although Coretta knew that Martin was in serious condition, seeing him came as a jolt. Weak and exhausted, Martin had drainage tubes in his nose and throat. Medication had made him drowsy, but his spirits rose when he saw Coretta. She stayed with Martin throughout his recovery.

IN GANDHI'S FOOTSTEPS

Martin longed to know more about his hero, the Indian political and spiritual leader Mohandas Gandhi. Martin considered Gandhi to be the inspiration behind African Americans' nonviolent protests. For a long time, Martin had wanted to visit India and speak with people who had known Gandhi. As Martin slowly regained strength, it seemed a good time to make the trip.

Coretta and Martin flew to India in March 1959. The Indian people welcomed the Kings warmly. Their first night in India, Coretta and Martin dined with Prime Minister Jawaharlal Nehru. The next day they met some of the key figures who had led the fight to free India, a British colony from the 1700s until 1947. Throughout their stay in India, the Kings talked with many people who had been followers of Gandhi.

The poverty the Kings encountered saddened them greatly. However, other aspects of India were inspiring. The prominent role of women in Indian politics fascinated Coretta. She believed it was important for all women to take greater roles in politics and government.

Everywhere the Kings went, Martin made speeches. The Indian people were anxious to hear all about the U.S. civil rights movement. Martin spoke to overflowing crowds. Usually Coretta joined her husband on the speaker's platform. She conveyed the soul of the move- ment through the African American spirituals she sang. Audiences were deeply moved by her singing. When the

Kings returned home, they were ready to continue Gandhi's nonviolent approach to civil rights.

LEAVING MONTGOMERY

Soon the Kings settled back into their hectic routines. Coretta wished that she could become more involved in the growing movement, but she had her hands full taking care of Yoki and Marty and running the household. Sometimes she wondered why Martin had to spend quite so much time away from his family. Couldn't he delegate some of his responsibility? But she supported her husband in everything he did, and she didn't complain about the amount of time he spent traveling.

As Martin devoted more time to civil rights, he worried that he wasn't doing enough for his congregation at Dexter Avenue Baptist Church. In November 1959, Martin decided to leave Montgomery and move to Atlanta. He had been traveling frequently to Atlanta since the SCLC was located there. The move would give him more time to spend with his family and allow the Dexter Baptist Church to have a full-time pastor again. Martin would join his father as copastor of Atlanta's Ebenezer Baptist Church.

ANOTHER TRIAL

The early days in Atlanta were hard on Coretta. Shortly after the move, Martin was accused of lying on his Alabama state income tax forms for 1956 and 1958. Coretta did everything she could to convince Martin that no one would believe the false charges. However, she could see that her husband was seriously troubled. He thought that the trumped-up charges were a deliberate attempt to discredit him and the entire civil rights movement. Seeing him so upset was difficult for Coretta.

The Kings returned to Montgomery in May 1960 for the trial. Martin was not optimistic. Twelve white men were chosen as jurors. Coretta steeled herself for the worst. To her amazement and joy, the verdict came back as not guilty.

Coretta had been so emotionally involved in the trial that she hadn't given much thought to her next task. Although she was usually busy at home, occasionally organizations invited her to share her outlook on the civil rights movement. On May 28, the day after the verdict, she was scheduled to speak at a church in Cleveland, Ohio. While her husband returned home from Montgomery, she traveled directly to Cleveland with Ralph Abernathy. They arrived at five o'clock in the morning. Exhausted, Coretta tried to get some rest, but she couldn't fall asleep. She kept thinking about recent events and worrying because she hadn't finished her speech.

But when Coretta stood before the congregation later that day, her worries fell away. She knew exactly what to say. Forgetting about her notes, she described Martin's trial, her fears, and her thankfulness for the positive outcome. Her directness and honesty appealed to listeners. The audience was captivated.

Marty and Yoki join their parents at the family piano in 1960.

Chapter FIVE

GROWING FAMILY AND EXPANDING MOVEMENT

CORETTA **FOUND HERSELF SPENDING MORE TIME ON** her own as Martin traveled around the country giving speeches. It became harder to stay home while she longed to do more for the movement. But being a mother came first for Coretta. A firm but loving parent, she did not want to spend prolonged periods of time away from her children. And by the middle of 1960, Coretta was expecting another baby.

A NEW FORM OF PROTEST

Meanwhile, more young people were joining the civil rights movement and taking it in a courageous new direction. On February 2, 1960, four African American college students sat down at a whites-only lunch counter in Greensboro, North Carolina. They knew their action could lead to their arrest. But they were determined to fight segregation. Less than one month later, sit-ins like this had been staged in fifteen cities. Everywhere, African Americans were seating themselves in whites-only areas and refusing to budge. By October, 112 southern cities had witnessed sit-ins.

One day Martin decided to join seventy-five students at a sit-in at an Atlanta department store. Coretta would have liked to accompany him, but Martin did not want her to run the risk of arrest. As it turned out, everyone who took part in the sit-in was taken to jail. Martin and most of the other protesters refused to post bond. They opted to stay in jail instead because it created more attention and sympathy for their cause.

Yoki and Marty missed their father. They wanted to know why he went to jail. Coretta gave them the truth in simple words they could understand. She said that their daddy had gone to jail to help people.

Despite the confident manner she kept up for Yoki and Marty, Coretta worried while Martin was in jail. Soon an agreement was reached to free the sit-in demonstrators. Anticipating a happy reunion, Coretta went to the restaurant where a celebration was being held. But Martin was nowhere in sight. Upon investigation, she learned that he had been kept in jail on a previous traffic technicality. Months earlier, Martin had been released on probation for driving with an invalid license—he hadn't replaced his Alabama license with a

Georgia license after moving to Atlanta. Taking part in the sit-in, officials said, was violating his probation. Coretta was disappointed and alarmed. She knew that the real reason Martin had been detained was to punish him for his strong stand on civil rights.

Coretta was surrounded by family and friends when she attended Martin's hearing. But she was not prepared for the guilty verdict he received and his sentence of six months of hard labor. Coretta burst into tears. Their baby would be born while Martin was still in jail.

Coretta did her best to remain strong. That night, however, Martin was transferred to a state prison 300 miles (483 km) from Atlanta. Coretta felt desperate. She knew he might be taunted, mistreated, or even killed there.

As Coretta was preparing to consult a lawyer, the telephone rang. Senator and presidential candidate John F. Kennedy wanted to talk to her. Coretta knew his voice well from the TV news. "I'm thinking about you and your husband," said Kennedy. "I know this must be a very difficult time for you. If there's anything I can do to help, I want you to please feel free to call me." A grateful Coretta said she would appreciate any help the senator could give. The next day, Coretta received news that Martin would be freed on bail. She took Yoki and Marty to the airport to greet their father when he returned to Atlanta on a chartered plane. (Kennedy later won his bid to become president.)

Marty, Yoki, and Coretta met Martin at the airport after he was released from Georgia State prison. He had been jailed for leading a sit-in at the lunch counter in an Atlanta department store.

PROTECTING HER CHILDREN

The stress Coretta endured during her pregnancy may have contributed to the premature birth of her son. Dexter Scott was born at the end of January 30, 1961, six weeks early. By this time, Yoki was five and Marty was three. Coretta kept busy caring for her three children. She did everything in her power to shield them from racism and bigotry.

Although Yoki and Marty were still too young to know about segregation, Coretta knew that before long they would begin to ask questions. Already Yoki was asking to stop at the playgrounds they passed in the car. Coretta always made up excuses. She couldn't bear to tell her daughter that the playgrounds were for white children only.

Yoki seemed to accept her mother's excuses about the playgrounds, she couldn't let go of one request. On television she saw commercials for an amusement park called Funtown. She could hardly wait to go there. Her parents were forced to invent excuse after excuse in response to Yoki's pleas. Finally, the frustrated six-year-old accused her parents of not wanting to take her to Funtown.

This was the conversation Coretta had been dreading. Gently, Coretta explained that African Americans were not welcome at Funtown. When Yoki started to cry, Coretta found herself using the same words her own mother had used many years earlier. She assured Yoki that she was as good as anyone else. Then Coretta explained that Yoki's daddy was working to change things so that people of all colors could go anywhere they wanted.

PEACE TALKS IN SWITZERLAND

In the meantime, both Coretta and Martin had been working hard. In addition to civil rights, Coretta was deeply committed to world peace. In March of 1962, an organization called the Women's Strike for Peace invited Coretta to go to Geneva, Switzerland. There they would attend a series of talks about banning the testing of atomic bombs. The women hoped their presence would underscore the urgent need to halt such tests. This would be the first step toward elimination of atomic weapons. Coretta became one of fifty

American women traveling to Geneva. Four of them were African American.

Like the other women, Coretta was concerned about the effects that weapons testing had on children. Explosions of atomic bombs in the open air could imperil children's health.

Coretta had a strong faith in the women of the world. She knew that race and nationality did not matter when the future of children was at stake. Women needed to stand firm in their demands for peace and safety for all people.

CRISIS IN BIRMINGHAM

By the spring of 1963, Martin and the SCLC had turned their attention to Birmingham, Alabama. Birmingham had a reputation among civil rights leaders as the "worst big city in the U.S.A."[8] Rather than obey a federal court order to integrate public facilities, the city had closed down playgrounds and parks, as well as six swimming pools and four golf courses.

Once again, Martin was forced to spend a great deal of time away from home. This was especially hard on Coretta because she was expecting another baby. On March 28, 1963, Martin drove her to the hospital, and Bernice Albertine (nicknamed Bunny) was born. The next day, Martin had to leave for Birmingham. When it was time for Coretta and the baby to go home, he hurried back so he could drive them himself. But within hours, Martin was on the road again, heading back to Birmingham. Coretta felt happy at the birth of her child and anxious for Martin's safety. She knew he might be jailed yet again. With a new baby to care for, she would not be able to visit him much.

Little Bernice was less than a month old when Martin disobeyed a state court order that prohibited protesters from marching in Birmingham. On April 12, the Friday before Easter, Martin led a march toward downtown Birmingham. He was arrested with Ralph Abernathy and about fifty other protesters. At the jail, Martin was locked in solitary confinement.

Meanwhile, Coretta was anxiously waiting to hear from her husband. For the first time in many years, she was not able to attend Easter Sunday church services. She was at home, waiting for Martin's call and trying to find a way to reach him. In desperation, Coretta finallly called President Kennedy.

When the president returned her call, he said that he had sent the FBI into Birmingham and that her husband was all right. Shortly after their conversation,

John F. Kennedy was the thirty-fifth president of the United States. His kindness to the King family while still a U.S. senator may have helped him win the presidential election in 1960.

the phone rang again. This time it was Martin. A thankful Coretta felt that her nightmare was ending. She finally got a chance to visit her husband two days before he was released on bond.

THE CHILDREN'S CRUSADE

Soon civil rights leaders came up with a powerful new tactic to gain support. They would recruit students and children to march for desegregation. Coretta's thoughts must have flown to Yoki, Marty, Dexter, and Bunny when she heard the news. Pitting children against the Birmingham police was a drastic measure. But the children were certain to capture the public's attention.

The children who marched in Birmingham showed immense courage. On May 2, 1963, the first day of the crusade, 959 children were taken to jail. The second

Police arrested children and teens during the Children's Crusade in May 1963.

day, more than one thousand children marched. Police Commissioner Eugene "Bull" Connor was determined to put an end to their protest. He unleashed police dogs and told firefighters to train their high-pressure hoses on the children. National television coverage showed children crumpling under the force of the gushing water and scrambling frantically to get away from the dogs. The public outrage was boundless. The resulting furor forced Birmingham businesspeople to give in to the marchers' demands. They pledged to integrate lunch counters and to employ black workers.

The Kings rejoiced over the agreement. They knew that once they had gained rights in Birmingham, they could anticipate more gains in other cities.

But Birmingham was still seething with hatred. Angry whites set off two bombs. One hit the home of Martin's brother. Riots erupted as African Americans retaliated. Police rushed to disperse the rioters. Martin and other civil rights leaders pleaded for an end to the violence. Although people responded to his message of peace, it wasn't until President Kennedy sent federal troops to nearby Fort McClellan that the crisis really ended. At last, Birmingham began a new era of integration. In addition, the civil rights movement gained a new momentum that would lead to more victories and would inspire President Kennedy to propose civil rights legislation.

In 1963 Coretta was ready to make civil rights a national issue.

Chapter **SIX**

WE SHALL OVERCOME

UNTIL THE SUMMER OF **1963,** CIVIL RIGHTS marches had been confined to individual cities. Like many others in the movement, Coretta believed it was time for a bold new move—a march that would draw people from the entire country. The success in Birmingham had inspired countless individuals. Surely, Coretta reasoned, they would respond to a call to march on Washington, D.C. She believed such a march would raise support for national legislation to fully integrate African Americans into society. President Kennedy already was calling for a civil rights law. The marchers would send a powerful message to Congress and to all Americans: "Pass the bill."

Coordinating the event was a tremendous undertaking. As Bayard Rustin, the director, pointed out, "We wanted to get everybody from the whole country, into Washington by nine o'clock in the morning and out of Washington by sundown." He had to map out a route and provide for the marchers' physical needs. Every detail had to be thought out carefully. But in the end, all the hard work was worth it. Marchers, including 60,000 white people, streamed into Washington aboard freedom trains and freedom buses.

MARCHING ON WASHINGTON

As Coretta traveled with Martin to Washington the day before the march, she knew he was concerned about his speech. That night, as she fell asleep in the hotel room, Martin continued to work. The next day, the Kings found the city teeming with people. With the massive crowd, Coretta made her way to the Lincoln Memorial. She sat behind her husband on the speaker's platform. Two hundred and fifty thousand people stood before her, stretching as far as her eyes could see. The tremendous turnout thrilled her.

When Martin stepped to the podium, he began the speech that he had rehearsed with Coretta. Then something happened. Moved by the sight of so many people united in a single cause, he set his notes aside. A vision of the future was taking shape in his mind, and he had to share it. Martin's words became one of the most famous speeches in U.S. history. He spoke of

Within sight of the Washington Monument (top center) *in Washington, D.C., Martin addressed the crowd during the March on Washington on August 23, 1963.*

his dream—a dream in which there would be no distinction between the descendants of former slaves and the descendants of former slave owners. Someday, he declared fervently, people of all races and religions would stand together, singing the powerful African American spiritual, "Free at last! Free at last! Thank God Almighty, we are free at last!"

When Martin was done, the crowd remained as silent as if they were in a cathedral. Then a mighty roar went up as the men and women voiced their profound agreement. Coretta never forgot the hope and the faith the vast crowd expressed, united in their longing for Martin's glorious dream.

TRAGEDY

That shining moment of unity and peace proved brief indeed. Three weeks after the march, a bomb exploded in a Baptist church in Birmingham. Four black girls died in the blast, prompting cries of grief and outrage.

HISTORIC WORDS: "I HAVE A DREAM"

Martin Luther King Jr. knew how to convey a strong message to his audience. His stirring delivery gave an added dimension to his powerful words. You can read, hear, or even watch Martin's most famous addresses, including his "I Have a Dream" speech from the March on Washington, at the following websites:

http://www.americanrhetoric.com/speeches/mlkihaveadream.htm

http://seattletimes.nwsource.com/mlk/king/speeches.html

http://www.drmartinlutherkingjr.com/

Two months later, the assassination of President Kennedy stunned the nation. Coretta grieved deeply for the man who had helped her husband during his darkest hours. As Martin watched the TV coverage, he quietly stated that he expected to have the same fate as Kennedy. All Coretta could do was hold his hand and move closer. She had a terrible fear that he might be right.

FULL OF PRIDE

The civil rights bill that Kennedy had championed did not die with him. Within days of Kennedy's death, the new president, Lyndon Johnson, declared the Civil

Rights Act the first priority of his administration. After a prolonged battle in the U.S. Senate, the bill was passed in July 1964. President Johnson invited Dr. King to the White House to see the bill signed into law.

Around this time, Coretta received a phone call from the Associated Press. Martin had been awarded the Nobel Peace Prize for 1964. Coretta's mind reeled. Moments later she was calling her husband. Playfully she asked how the Nobel Peace Prizewinner was doing. In December, Coretta accompanied Martin to Oslo, Norway, to receive the award. Listening to her husband's acceptance speech, Coretta couldn't help but feel immensely proud of him.

Day by Day

Martin was proud of Coretta too. She was instilling commitment, courage, and confidence in their children. She also helped them deal with the attention they drew as the family of Martin Luther King Jr. Tired of the spotlight, Yoki told her classmates one day that she wanted to be treated like everyone else. That was what Coretta wanted for her children too. She did everything possible to keep their lives ordinary. She took them to visit her parents' farm. She applauded the plays that Yoki, who loved acting, staged with Marty, Dexter, and Bunny. She also shared her love of music. Coretta played the piano and sang with her husband and children as often as possible.

Coretta still yearned to do more for civil rights. She wanted to be able to accept more speaking engagements and to join Martin on marches. But Martin, like many men of his generation, felt that Coretta's place was at home, taking care of the children. Sometimes Coretta felt left out and frustrated. She wondered why her husband couldn't understand her need to serve. Occasionally they argued. But the love and commitment that bound them together never wavered.

FREEDOM CONCERTS

Finally Coretta found an outlet for her creativity and a unique way to help the civil rights movement. In late 1964, she gave the first in a series of Freedom Concerts to raise money for the SCLC. Singing and speaking, she told "The Story of the Struggle from 1955 to 1965," as she and Martin had lived it. She talked about the Montgomery Bus Boycott and the March on Washington. She poured all her hope, longing, and faith into the words as she sang such inspiring pieces as "He's Got the Whole World in His Hands" and "We Shall Overcome." Her courage and beautiful voice enthralled audiences. Coretta earned more than $50,000 for the movement.

MARCHING IN SELMA

Coretta was giving a Freedom Concert in San Francisco when she learned of a confrontation between civil rights marchers and the police in Selma, Alabama. The city employed various means to prevent black citizens from registering to vote. To raise awareness of the unfair voting system, six hundred marchers planned to walk all the way from Selma to the state capital of Montgomery.

But, when the marchers arrived at the Edmund Pettus Bridge, on the outskirts of Selma, police halted their progress. They beat the demonstrators with clubs. Mounted on horses, police officers plunged headlong into the crowd of marchers, sending them scrambling for safety. The terrifying scene made the national news. The day became known as Bloody Sunday. Across the nation, people were horrified.

BIGOTRY IN VOTER REGISTRATION

lthough the U.S. Constitution guarantees all Americans the right to vote, many southern towns devised ways to prevent African Americans from exercising that right. Some local governments demanded literacy tests that were designed for African Americans to fail. In other towns, voter registration offices made black people stand in line for hours, then closed abruptly without registering everyone. Some states charged poll taxes. Many African Americans could not afford to pay the fee to vote.

Martin and Coretta were determined to end such illegal practices. When black citizens could go freely to the polls, they would be able to vote bigoted officials out of office.

Two days after Bloody Sunday, Martin led protestors back across the bridge in Selma. Protestors knelt in prayer on the far side of the bridge, but the police (right) were ready for trouble.

Martin had not been in Selma at the time of the march. But he telephoned Coretta to say he was going to Selma to lead another demonstration. Coretta knew the situation was fraught with danger. However, she couldn't let her worries overcome her. The justice of her cause gave her courage.

Two days later, Martin led fifteen hundred marchers back to the Edmund Pettus Bridge, where they sang "We Shall Overcome." Afterward, they knelt in prayer before the armed troopers. Rising at last, Martin halted the march, and the people turned back. Many were disappointed by this unexpected end to their protest. But Martin wanted to avoid more senseless violence.

TRIUMPHANT HOMECOMING

Martin waited until a court order prohibiting the march was lifted. Then he rallied the people to begin the 54-mile (87 km) march to the capital once more.

Four thousand marchers set off on Sunday, March 21, 1965. Coretta was scheduled to speak that day in Greensboro, North Carolina. She joined the marchers on Monday. On Tuesday she made a quick trip to Atlanta to check on her children. The next day, she flew back to Montgomery and rejoined the march. That evening they camped out on the grounds of St. Jude's Hospital, the same hospital where Coretta's first two children had been born. Celebrities who were marching, including Harry Belafonte and Sammy Davis Jr., performed for the crowd. Then Coretta was asked to say a few words.

Coretta stood on the lit platform, surrounded by darkness. She told her listeners how meaningful it felt to be back in Montgomery, ten years after moving there with her husband. She also read a poignant poem by African American writer Langston Hughes.

Throughout the night, people kept arriving to join the final trek into downtown Montgomery. Coretta was deeply moved as the throngs marched triumphantly into the city. To her delight, she spied her mother and father standing not far from the state capitol building. Hurriedly she made arrangements for them to be seated on the platform when the speeches began. Coretta felt that her father spoke for all the marchers when he called that day the greatest moment in history for African Americans.

President Lyndon B. Johnson (seated) *signs the Civil Rights Act of 1964* (above), *while Martin* (behind the president) *and other civil rights supporters watched. Johnson went on to sign the Voting Rights Act in 1965.*

Chapter **SEVEN**

FIGHTING WAR AND POVERTY

TWO SIGNIFICANT EVENTS HAPPENED IN THE SUMMER of 1965. First, on August 6, President Johnson signed the Voting Rights Act into law. States could no longer use literacy tests or any other method to deny African Americans their constitutional right to vote.

The second important event was the integration of Atlanta's public schools. This finally came eleven years after the Supreme Court had ruled that segregation had no place in education. Coretta was eager for Yoki and Marty to attend integrated schools. But the children did not like the idea of being the only African Americans in a school that had previously been just for whites. Coretta solved the problem by sending them to the same school as Ralph Abernathy's children. Although the school wanted as little publicity as possible, the press considered the King children's integrated schooling to be a top news item. Coretta spoke to reporters because she wanted to show that black and white youngsters could attend school together in harmony. She hoped her example would prompt other African Americans to enroll their children in formerly white schools.

THE VIETNAM WAR

As Yoki and Marty adjusted to their new school, Coretta and Martin were confronting another major issue—the war in Vietnam. The United States was sending troops into the small Southeast Asian nation in an effort to prevent Communists from taking it over. Some people questioned whether this was an appropriate action for the government to take, especially as casualties mounted. Other people supported the war, believing that Communism must be stopped, whatever the cost. The United States was sharply divided.

Coretta believed firmly that the war was wrong. Even before Martin voiced his own opposition, Coretta spoke out against the buildup of troops in Vietnam. On November 27, 1965, a huge antiwar rally was held in Washington, D.C. Standing by the Washington Monument, Coretta addressed a crowd of thirty thousand. She declared that America's greatest strength lay in its democracy. Just as with civil rights, she believed that if enough people voiced their opposition to the war, the government would have to listen.

THE NEXT STEP

As the number of U.S. soldiers in Vietnam rose, Coretta and Martin continued to speak out. They not only felt the war was unjust, they also believed it diverted funds that should be used to help poor people. Instead of spending money on weapons, the Kings thought the government should use its resources to eliminate poverty. Poverty, not Communism, trapped many African Americans in dangerous ghettos. Poverty gave rise to despair, rage, and rioting. Poverty led to de facto segregation in cities such as Chicago, Illinois, that had no segregation laws.

Coretta and Martin believed that the next step in the fight for equality was to secure economic opportunity for all people. Then more African Americans would be able to afford good housing, and neighborhoods would become integrated. Martin and the SCLC launched a crusade in Chicago to secure social and economic justice for ghetto dwellers. In order to share the plight of the poor, Martin rented an apartment in one of the city's worst slums. Coretta and Martin walked up three flights of rickety stairs in almost total darkness. The smell of urine penetrated the hallways. The apartment itself was cramped, cold, and noisy.

Coretta spent a great deal of time with Martin in his dingy surroundings, traveling back and forth to take care of the children. When school was out, she brought Yoki, Marty, Dexter, and Bunny to Chicago too. Although she hated to see her children in such gloomy

Martin and Coretta wave from the center window of their third-floor apartment in a Chicago slum.

circumstances, Coretta felt it was worthwhile for them to understand firsthand how poor people lived.

CONFRONTING RIOTS

On Sunday, July 19, 1966, a rally was held in Chicago. All four King children marched with their family, although Bunny had to be carried after the first few blocks. Martin nailed a sheet of paper listing his demands for economic and social justice to the door of city hall. It was an act reminiscent of history's Martin Luther, leader of the Protestant Reformation. In 1517 Luther had nailed his protests against corruption in the Catholic Church to a church door in Germany.

The next day, Martin discussed his demands with Chicago mayor Richard Daley. When the mayor refused to consider them, rioting broke out. Coretta spent that night roaming the streets with Martin, trying to lessen the tension between angry youths and the police.

The next day, Coretta spoke at the YWCA. She proposed that better economic conditions might help prevent further street warfare. Someone suggested that a telegram be sent to Mayor Daley in support of Martin's demands. Coretta encouraged women to sign their names to such a telegram, even if they feared that identifying themselves—and, thus, their families—would jeopardize their husbands' jobs with the city. The time had come to take action, she argued.

The women were convinced. They decided to send the telegram. They also decided to create a woman's organization, suggested by Coretta, that would push for Dr. King's economic reforms.

Meanwhile, the violence continued. Coretta took her children with her the next evening when she spoke to a small group. As they were driven home, Coretta heard gunshots and saw shards of broken glass littering the sidewalks. Once back at the apartment, the children raced to the window to see where the shots were coming from. Anxiously, Coretta screamed at them to get away before they were seen and shot.

For much of the night, Coretta lay awake in bed, listening to shots and to glass shatter. Although she was frightened for her children's safety, she was also saddened. The rioters had good reason to be upset, she knew, but they were expressing their frustration in ways that endangered themselves and others.

POOR PEOPLE'S CAMPAIGN

Not long after the violence ended, Coretta returned to Atlanta with her children. The sixties were a time of great social upheaval as people continued fighting for civil rights and opposing the Vietnam War. Some African Americans felt that nonviolent protest did not get results quickly enough. Many who lived in the squalor of ghettos and dire poverty despaired. In the summer of 1967, rioting broke out in several major cities.

Martin had an idea that he hoped would quell the riots. He would bring poor people of all races together to march in Washington, D.C. They would take their demands for jobs and financial security directly to the U.S. government. To make their presence truly felt, they would set up a camp on the Washington Mall (a large park in the center of the city). The hardships of the poor would be visible to the entire nation.

While he was still planning that great campaign for the summer of 1968, Martin also became involved in the plight of sanitation workers in Memphis, Tennessee. Police had used violence to end a demonstration by employees, most of them black, who had gone on strike for better working conditions. The police beat strikers with clubs and sprayed them with mace. People were shocked by the savage reaction to a peaceful march.

FBI SURVEILLANCE

Coretta and Martin didn't have a perfect marriage. Illegal recordings of Dr. King's private conversations, made by J. Edgar Hoover, the head of the FBI, indicate that Martin was not always a faithful husband. Whatever anger or distress Coretta might have felt, she rose above it. She loved her husband and was certain of his love for her. Her unwavering support meant a great deal to Martin.

Martin recognized that the sanitation workers were simply trying to earn a decent living. Sympathetic, he addressed a mass meeting in Memphis and agreed to lead a protest march through the city. When violence erupted during the march, Martin was devastated. He wanted to show that peaceful demonstrations were still possible and effective. He agreed to lead another march in Memphis to help the striking workers.

Martin's family felt uneasy. Although Bunny was too young to understand what was happening, the three oldest King children didn't want their father to go to Memphis. Coretta must have sensed her children's worries. As usual, she must have tried to soothe their anxieties. Perhaps she too had forebodings about Memphis. But she would not ask Martin to stay home when his conscience urged him forward.

Coretta stands next to a photo of Martin.

Chapter **EIGHT**

LEARNING TO FORGIVE

WHEN MARTIN RETURNED TO MEMPHIS, HE MADE one of the most moving speeches of his career. Using biblical language, Martin said he had glimpsed the promised land that African Americans were struggling to reach. He knew that, as a people, they would achieve their goals. What he didn't know was whether he would live to share that fulfillment with them.

Meanwhile, Coretta and the children went about their daily lives. On Thursday, April 4, Coretta spent a pleasant day shopping for Easter clothes with Yoki. Shortly after she arrived home, Reverend Jesse Jackson called with news that changed her life forever. Martin Luther King Jr. had been shot. An ambulance had rushed him to the hospital.

Coretta was numb with shock, even though she wasn't really surprised. On some level, she had been expecting this call for a long time. All she could do was say that she would fly to Memphis at once.

Dexter and Marty found their mother on the phone while she was still talking to Reverend Jackson. They knew from a news bulletin on television that something had happened to their father. Coretta told them he had been shot. Seven-year-old Dexter asked repeatedly how soon his dad would be home.

Staying calm for her children had become a way of life for Coretta. Quietly she explained that she was going to Memphis to see Martin. She promised to call Dexter after she arrived.

When Coretta was almost ready to board her plane, she heard her name over the airport loudspeaker. She froze. Moments later, the mayor of Atlanta found Coretta and spoke the words she dreaded. Her husband was dead. Crying, Coretta prepared to return to her children. She tried to think of how to give them the news.

Yoki already knew by the time her mother arrived home. Confused and distraught, she wanted to know if she should hate the man responsible for her father's death.

Heartbroken, Coretta replied that Martin would never want his children to hate anyone—not even the man who had killed him. They must learn to forgive. That had always been their father's philosophy, and she wanted them to embrace it.

But the shock and grief of some African Americans spilled over into rage. They wanted revenge for the death of their beloved leader. Rioting broke out in major cities. Hoping to stem the violence, Coretta pulled herself together and called a press conference. She urged the rioters to restrain themselves. She reminded people that her husband had opposed violence under all circumstances and that he had died seeking a peaceful way to effect social change.

THE NATION MOURNS

All over the country, people were stunned by the death of Martin Luther King Jr. Friends and supporters showered Coretta and the children with kindness. President Johnson and Senator Robert Kennedy (John Kennedy's brother) phoned to offer their condolences. Jacqueline Kennedy (John Kennedy's widow) and Richard Nixon went to Atlanta to express their sympathy in person. But as Coretta noted later, no one could lessen the burden of those intense hours of grief.

The march Martin had planned to lead was still scheduled for April 8. That morning Coretta flew to Memphis with her three oldest children. They joined the throng of marchers about 1 mile (1.6 km) from the city hall. Coretta thought there might have been as many as fifty thousand people. Yet it was a very silent crowd. Many people were dressed in mourning and carried signs bearing Martin's name. Some wept openly. After the march, Coretta addressed the masses. She reminded

On April 8, 1968, Coretta (third from right) *and other family members led Martin's Memphis march. It was the day before his funeral.*

mourners that her husband's spirit would never die. She challenged them to continue his work.

Ebenezer Baptist Church was packed for Martin's funeral the next day. Tens of thousands of people lined the streets outside the church to hear the service broadcast over loudspeakers. A mule-drawn wagon carried the casket to Morehouse College, Martin, where he had received his first college degree. There he was laid to rest. Mourners filled the streets as they accompanied Martin on his final march. Coretta dedicated herself to her children and to the civil rights movement from that point on.

ON HER OWN

When she woke up each morning to life without her husband, Coretta cried. Then she dried her tears and prepared to face the day with her children. It was up to her to provide strength and stability for her family. She filled their days with activities so they would be too busy to dwell on their grief.

Coretta also had to think about how to support her family. Martin had left her little beyond their home. Coretta had about five thousand dollars, plus income from an insurance policy that her friend, the entertainer Harry Belafonte, had taken out for the family on Martin's life. She also earned royalties on an autobiography she wrote. Through the years, Coretta made ends meet mostly from the fees she received for making speeches. But she might charge for only two or three of the many public appearances she made each month. She admitted it wasn't always easy to pay the bills.

PROTESTING THE WAR

On her forty-first birthday, April 27, 1968, Coretta took Martin's place at an antiwar rally held in New York's Central Park. The number of U.S. casualties in Vietnam continued to rise. Many innocent Vietnamese civilians also died. Coretta had found some notes that she believed Martin had intended to use in giving his speech at this rally. She read his "Ten Commandments on Vietnam" to the crowd. Most of the commandments admonished people not to believe everything they read about

Coretta addresses the crowd in Resurrection City, Washington, D.C., in 1968.

the war. The last one echoed one of the biblical Ten Commandments—simply, "Thou shalt not kill."

RESURRECTION CITY

Several days later, on May 2, Coretta stood on the same Memphis balcony where her husband had been shot. Below her, people waited to march. It was time to begin the Poor People's Campaign, to which Martin had been so dedicated. Coretta joined the marchers after a brief speech. They made their way through the city's slums, singing "We Shall Overcome."

Over the next week, poor people poured into Washington, D.C. For over a month, they lived in tents on the vast mall stretching between the U.S. Capitol and the Lincoln Memorial. The encampment was called Resurrection City.

Coretta made several trips to Washington with her children during the campaign. They visited Vice President Hubert Humphrey in the White House. They also went to Resurrection City, where Coretta called upon her sisters of all races and ethnic groups to come together to fight racism, poverty, and war.

MORE TRAGEDY

Before Resurrection City had broken up, the nation faced another tragedy. Robert Kennedy, a candidate for the Democratic nomination for president, had been assassinated in Los Angeles. Kennedy had always been a friend to the Kings. Just two months earlier, he had marched in Martin's funeral procession. Coretta flew to California to offer heartfelt condolences to Kennedy's wife. First John F. Kennedy, next Martin Luther King, and then Robert Kennedy had been struck down. The world seemed unspeakably dangerous and tragic.

As Coretta sat through the funeral, a message was handed to her. Police in London, England, had arrested James Earl Ray, the man suspected of killing her husband. Coretta opposed the death penalty. Even when Ray pleaded guilty to murder, she did not want him to die. Because of his guilty plea, Ray's trial was short. He was sentenced to ninety-nine years in prison.

A NEW FOCUS

Grief did not slow down Coretta. To help keep Martin's legacy alive, she decided to create a center that would be a living memorial to him. She envisioned a great research library and a training facility where people could come to learn about nonviolent approaches to social change. She would name it after her husband: The

Martin Luther King Jr. Memorial Center. Coretta hoped that the SCLC would help create the center. The leaders of the SCLC, however, did not support Coretta's plan. They felt that their organization's funds could be better used in other ways. Some members even questioned if Martin himself would have liked the idea.

Coretta was disappointed but undaunted. She began to establish the center in the basement of her house. But it was a long time before the enterprise was open to the public. First Coretta needed to raise funds and purchase land. She needed to develop workshops and other projects to further her husband's goals. As much as possible, Coretta included her children in her work. As she publicized her plans, many famous people offered their support. Organizations across the country invited her to speak.

FAMILY FIRST

Although her days were hectic, Coretta always put her family first. She told her assistants to interrupt her, no matter what she was doing, if the children ever needed her. One day Coretta was talking to President Ronald Reagan when her assistant signaled that her daughter Bernice was on the other line. Immediately Coretta said good-bye to the president and took her daughter's call.

Coretta knew that her children were under a great deal of pressure to live up to their father's legacy. She told them that they did not have to be what others expected them to be but should create their own pathways through life. And she made sure Marty knew that he did not have to become a minister or follow in his father's footsteps. All he had to do was be the best person he could be.

BRINGING HOPE TO THE WORLD

After Coretta announced her plans for the King Center early in 1969, she set off on an important trip. On March 16, 1969, she became the first woman to give a speech at St. Paul's Cathedral in London. Despite the violence and unrest in the world, she told the audience that she believed a new order was emerging. She then went on to Rome, where she had a private audience with the Roman Catholic leader, Pope Paul VI.

Coretta continued her travels from there. Several years earlier, she had visited India with Martin and dined with Prime Minister Nehru. She returned to the country alone in 1969 to accept the Nehru Award for International Understanding on behalf of her husband. The honor included an award of $13,000 (about 100,000 Indian rupees). Coretta donated half the prize money to the civil rights movement. She gave the rest to sponsor a student from India's lowest social class, the Untouchable caste, to come to the United States and study at the developing King Center. Untouchables endured terrible discrimination and hardship. Coretta wanted to do everything possible to help bring hope, dignity, and freedom to them and to all people.

Coretta wrote an autobiography titled, My Life with Martin Luther King Jr. It was published in 1969.

Chapter **NINE**

KEEPER OF THE DREAM

TRAGEDY CONTINUED TO HAUNT THE KING FAMILY. In 1969 Martin's brother, nicknamed A.D., drowned in a swimming pool. His family was bewildered. A.D. had been an excellent swimmer. Some people thought the circumstances surrounding his death were suspicious.

About five years later, Martin's mother, Alberta Williams King, was shot and killed as she sat playing the organ in Ebenezer Baptist Church. The entire family was devastated. But Daddy King reminded them that they must forgive even the man who killed her.

EMPLOYMENT ISSUES

Despite almost unbearable sorrow, Coretta never lost faith in the future. In 1974 Coretta began to address the issue of unemployment. Many African Americans were still having a hard time securing jobs. So Coretta founded the Full Employment Action Council. The council encouraged lawmakers to enact legislation that would lower unemployment.

The policy known as affirmative action represented another attempt to redress the imbalance between African American and white levels of employment. Affirmative action allowed employers and college entrance committees to give special consideration to blacks and other minorities. Coretta thought affirmative action was a good way to help disadvantaged people catch up with the rest of society. But some felt that it was unfair to other applicants. As challenges arose to affirmative action, Coretta defended the concept strongly.

She knew, though, that even more had to be done about unemployment. Too many people could not find decent, well-paying jobs. Too many families lived in substandard housing and could barely afford groceries. Coretta decided to highlight their struggles on her husband's birthday in 1976. Congress had not yet made Martin's birthday a national holiday. But the King Center held a special celebration on January 20. A march took place in Atlanta, with members of labor unions as the largest contingent. The march focused public attention on the urgent need to increase the employment rate and to improve working conditions.

President Jimmy Carter (right) *and his wife Rosalyn* (fourth from right) *join hands and sing with Coretta* (second from right) *and Martin Luther King Sr.* (left) *at Ebenezer Baptist Church in Atlanta, on January 14, 1979.*

POLITICS AND THE KING CENTER

Presidential candidate Jimmy Carter benefited from the 1976 celebration because he supported the demands of the unions. The marchers' votes may have helped him win the presidency that year. Coretta and Daddy King had also spoken out in favor of Carter. Many years later, a grateful Carter would state, "Each of their public handshakes to me was worth a million Yankee votes." Carter did not forget his political allies after the election. Ever since Martin's death, Coretta had been working to have his birthday declared a national holiday. President Carter endorsed her efforts. As a result, in 1979, Coretta testified before Congress in favor of the holiday.

It wasn't until 1983, however, when Carter was out of office, that the national holiday bill was signed into law. By that time, twenty years had passed since

Martin had given his famous "I Have a Dream" speech during the March on Washington. Coretta commemorated the anniversary by creating the Coalition of Conscience, which united eight hundred human rights groups in a huge demonstration in Washington. Half a million people participated, demanding that the government commit more resources to eliminating poverty.

The new King Center had also been completed by then, opening to the public in 1982. The Martin Luther King Jr. Center for Nonviolent Social Change was built in Sweet Auburn, a historically vibrant African American neighborhood of Atlanta. The complex had grown to include Freedom Hall (housing an auditorium, a resource center, and international artwork), a library and archives, and exhibits on Martin's life and work. In addition, Dr. King's grave had been moved to a new memorial on the grounds. The center offered programs and tours and classes to train people in the way of nonviolence.

Coretta had worked for years to raise enough money to fund the memorial project. Completing the center took millions of dollars in donations from individuals, foundations, and the federal government. The center's funding also allowed people to visit the King Center for free—there is no admission charge.

Coretta was proud of the King Center and expected top performance from the staff. She let someone know if she was dissatisfied with their job performance. A perfectionist, she was just as demanding of herself.

ANTIAPARTHEID

Coretta's concerns extended to the nation of South
Africa. The government there ruthlessly enforced
apartheid, the rigid separation of blacks and whites in
society. On June 26, 1985, she protested outside the
South African embassy in Washington, D.C. Despite public sympathy and respect, she was arrested with two of
her children, Martin III, then 26, and Bernice, 22.

The next year, Coretta traveled to South Africa to inves-
tigate conditions for herself. On September 11, 1986, she
met with Winnie Mandela, then wife of the imprisoned
antiapartheid leader Nelson Mandela. Both women had
made huge sacrifices for the cause of civil rights. Coretta
considered their meeting a highlight of her life.

When she returned home, Coretta urged President Reagan to enforce sanctions against South Africa. That
meant the United States would not trade with the country until all its citizens enjoyed the same freedoms.
Although Reagan felt that other means could be used to
stimulate reform in South Africa, Coretta's view was a
popular one. Congress voted to impose a ban on all
imports from the country. When Reagan vetoed the bill,
Congress overrode his action.

ALWAYS ON THE GO

As the years passed, Coretta broadened her platform to
embrace a host of issues. Tirelessly, she spoke out for
women's rights, civil rights for gays and lesbians, an end
to the nuclear arms race, and AIDS education. She also

passionately supported gun control. On April 4, 1993, the twenty-fifth anniversary of her husband's death, she spoke out forcefully against the easy availability of guns and their role in inner-city violence.

Wherever people were in need, Coretta wanted to help. In 1992 a severe hurricane ravaged Florida. The King Center sent three truckloads of food and supplies to the victims. But Coretta wanted to give more personal support too. She visited the scene of the devastation, knocking on doors and offering encouragement.

Coretta's goodwill missions took her all over the world. She traveled to Latin America, Europe, and Asia. Coretta loved to bring back souvenirs for her children. She was proud of their accomplishments as adults. Yolanda had become an actress. Martin III was involved with the King Center and the SCLC. Dexter was a businessman and also led the King Center for a time. Later he worked as an actor. Bernice received a law degree and became a minister.

Justice in South Africa

When Coretta returned to South Africa in 1994, the country's struggles against apartheid had wrought great changes. Laws discriminating against black Africans had been repealed. Many political prisoners, including Nelson Mandela, had been set free.

Coretta's visit coincided with the election in which Mandela won the presidency. She never forgot looking out from her hotel room to discover the cause of a

Coretta (background, left) *welcomed Nelson Mandela* (left of monument) *and his wife Winnie* (raising her fist) *to the King Center in Atlanta after Nelson's release from prison in 1990.*

strange, persistent buzzing. Huge numbers of people had gathered around the hotel, where Mandela himself was awaiting the official results. The noise that Coretta had heard was the people chanting his name over and over. Wanting to hear the results, she descended to the lobby. When Nelson Mandela spied her, he brought her onto the stage and hugged her.

As a means of proclaiming their joy, many South Africans, including Mandela, began performing a Zulu dance known as the *toi toi*. Coretta joined right in. She was so happy to be part of that moment.

DANGEROUS INCIDENT

As her seventieth birthday approached, Coretta, still vigorous and attractive, continued to live in the same home she had shared with her husband. Her son Dexter was getting concerned. Crime had been on the rise in the neighborhood.

In 1996 Coretta's home was burglarized during the night. The thief even took items from the bedroom where she was sleeping. Coretta woke up only as the robber made his exit. When the police captured him, they learned that he had committed three rapes and a murder. It may have been the recognition of Martin Luther King's widow that kept him from killing Coretta too. Dexter wanted to move his mother somewhere else at once. But Coretta declined. Despite the incident, she wanted to stay in her home.

Reopening the Past

Coretta showed a different kind of bravery when she came out in favor of a new trial for James Earl Ray, the man in prison for killing her husband. She felt there was evidence that Ray might have been framed and that perhaps the U.S. government had been involved. Although Ray had initially confessed to killing Martin Luther King, he had later changed his story. He had even claimed his innocence in a face-to-face meeting with Dexter Scott King. Coretta felt compelled to know the truth. In February 1997, she traveled to Memphis with Dexter. They testified in court that they felt the rifle Ray had allegedly used should undergo further tests.

Many people criticized them for trying to reopen what had been a closed case for years. The state of Tennessee resisted requests to conduct further investigation. Before the issue could be resolved, Ray died in 1998. It was too late for a new criminal trial. But the next year, Coretta filed a civil suit against a man named Loyd Jowers. Jowers had claimed in an interview several years earlier that he had taken part in the assassination.

Seventy witnesses were called before the court. Coretta was one of the first to testify. A month later, Dexter called her in Atlanta with the verdict. The jury had found Jowers guilty of conspiring with others, including government agencies, to kill Martin Luther King Jr.

However, few political analysts were willing to change their beliefs about the King assassination. Historians claimed that the new verdict was meaningless. Coretta and her children disagreed. They felt they finally had a clearer idea of what happened on April 4, 1968.

In 2003 Coretta attended the fortieth anniversary celebration of the 1963 March on Washington at the Lincoln Memorial.

TIME FOR SOME FUN

In 2003 Oprah Winfrey recruited Coretta to appear on an episode of her show devoted to makeovers. Coretta

WHAT FRIENDS HAVE SAID ABOUT CORETTA SCOTT KING

Oprah **Winfrey**, actress and TV personality: "She leaves us all better prepared to nurture, to strengthen, to broaden and deepen the democracy and human rights that she devoted her life to upholding."

Maya Angelou, poet: "African Americans and white Americans and Asians and Spanish-speaking—she belonged to us and that's a great thing."

Synthia Brown-Dyson, bodyguard and close friend: "She changed my life before I even knew it needed changing."

Reverend Bob Graetz, white minister in Montgomery during the bus boycott: "There were many days when Martin was close to the edge; she was an anchor for him."[23]

Maya Angelou and Coretta at the 1996 Initiatives for Women gala

had worn the same hairstyle for many years. At the last minute, she had second thoughts about getting her hair cut on national television. "You need to have a little fun," Oprah coaxed her. After the makeover, Coretta loved the way she looked.

Oprah was happy to do anything she could for Coretta. She helped convince her to move into a thirty-ninth-floor condominium. Oprah also took Coretta on a cruise with poet Maya Angelou. "I felt blessed, always, to be in [Coretta's] presence," Oprah later remembered.

SERVICE TO HUMANITY

In 2004 Coretta returned to Antioch College to celebrate her alma mater's 150th anniversary and to receive the prestigious Horace Mann Award. Many organizations had honored Coretta through the years, but this award was especially dear to her. Horace Mann, the first president of Antioch, had exhorted students to do something for the good of humanity before they died. For more than fifty years, Coretta had lived by his words. Accepting the award, she called for an end to violence and poverty and challenged her listeners to create a new world.

In her mid-seventies, Coretta had no intention of slowing down. She continued to travel and to champion important reforms. In early 2003, she spoke out against going to war with Iraq. And although she had turned over the running of the King Center to others, she maintained a deep involvement in all its programs.

FINAL DAYS

Coretta was beginning to feel her age by 2005. In August, she suffered a stroke that partially paralyzed her and left her unable to talk for a while. She was still extremely weak when her sister, Edythe, celebrated her eightieth birthday in November. Throughout their lives, the sisters had remained very close. Although Coretta was not able to attend the party or to speak distinctly yet, she managed to sing "Happy Birthday" to her sister over the speakerphone. It meant a great deal to Edythe and to everyone present.

Coretta's progress was slow. In addition to her heart condition, she was fighting ovarian cancer. The doctors had little hope for a full recovery. But Coretta refused to give up. On January 14, 2006, she made her first public appearance since her stroke. Coretta was greeted with a standing ovation at a Salute to Greatness dinner celebrating Martin Luther King Day in Atlanta. Leaning on her children, she rose from her wheelchair and waved to the crowd. To the assembled guests, she was a living legend, the very embodiment of the civil rights movement.

Two weeks later, on January 31, Coretta died at an alternative health clinic in Mexico where she had gone to seek treatment. The world mourned. Flags flew at half-mast on government buildings throughout her home state of Georgia.

Coretta was the first woman and first African American to lie in state in the Georgia state capitol. At her

Coretta's children (from left) *Martin III, Dexter, Yolanda, and Bernice stand beside the monument marking their parents' burial place at the King Center. Yolanda herself passed away in 2007.*

funeral, former president Jimmy Carter praised Coretta and Martin for the intensity and peacefulness with which they fought for equality and human dignity. Presidents George H. W. Bush, Bill Clinton, and George W. Bush also spoke. Bernice King, who had sat on her mother's lap at her father's funeral, gave the eulogy. She stressed that her mother never did anything for fame or for fortune. She simply followed God's plan for her life.

That is the way Coretta saw her destiny too. She once said that, even as a child, she knew she had a special purpose. As she worked for civil rights, developed the King Center, and championed vital causes, she never doubted that she had found her mission. Coretta Scott King inspired countless individuals all over the world to speak out for justice. Living each day with faith and courage, she helped forge a new world of increased racial harmony.

GLOSSARY

affirmative action: a government policy, also used by some colleges and employers, that gives special consideration or advantages to minority groups

apartheid: a former South African policy of rigid racial segregation in all areas of society

civil rights: rights to which every citizen of the United States is entitled under the Constitution

Civil Rights Act of 1964: a congressional act that withheld government funds from segregated schools or from any organizations that did not accord African Americans their full civil rights

civil rights movement: a campaign to ensure that African Americans and other minorities receive the same rights as white Americans

Coalition of Conscience: a coming together of eight hundred civil rights groups to Washington, D.C. It was organized by Coretta Scott King in 1983 to precipitate government action to help the poor.

Communism: system of government that outlaws private property and restricts freedom of speech and religion

de facto segregation: segregation due to socioeconomic conditions rather than local or state laws

desegregation: efforts to end segregation, allowing African Americans to enjoy their full civil rights

integration: the complete intermingling of African Americans and whites in all aspects of society

Jim Crow laws: a series of unconstitutional regulations enacted in the South, aimed to separate African

Americans from whites and to prevent African Americans from enjoying the full privileges of U.S. citizenship

literacy test: a biased reading test designed to prevent African Americans from voting

Montgomery Bus Boycott: the refusal of African Americans to use public transportation in Montgomery, Alabama, until the bus system was integrated

Montgomery Improvement Association (MIA): the civil rights organization that coordinated the Montgomery Bus Boycott

National Association for the Advancement of Colored People (NAACP): an organization dedicated to helping African Americans achieve their constitutional rights

poll tax: a measure aimed at preventing African Americans, many of whom could not afford the tax, from voting

Poor People's Campaign: an encampment of poor people in Washington, D.C., to draw the attention of Congress and the nation to the need to address the pressing problem of poverty

segregation: the separation of African Americans and whites in schools and public facilities

sit-ins: protests in which African American students refused to budge from lunch counters labeled "white only"

Southern Christian Leadership Conference (SCLC): an organization formed to further the gains made by the Montgomery Bus Boycott and to extend civil rights to all African Americans

Voting Rights Act: a congressional act outlawing poll taxes, literacy tests, and any other measure designed to deny African Americans their right to vote

Source Notes

8 Martin Luther King Jr., *The Autobiography of Martin Luther King, Jr.*, ed. Clayborne Carson (New York, Boston: IPM in association with Warner Books, 1988), 226.

24 Taylor Branch, *Parting the Waters: America in the King Years 1954–63* (New York: Simon & Schuster, 1988), 95–96.

33 Juan Williams, *Eyes on the Prize: America's Civil Rights Years, 1954–1965* (New York: Penguin Books, 2002), 68.

36 Ibid.

41 Martin Luther King Jr., 87.

46 Coretta Scott King, *My Life with Martin Luther King Jr.* (New York: Avon Books, 1979), 165.

53 Williams, 142.

56 Ibid., 179.

61 Ibid., 198.

62 Ibid.

63 Martin Luther King Jr., 226.

84 Octavia Vivian, *Coretta: The Story of Coretta Scott King*, Commemorative edition (Minneapolis: Fortress Press, 2006), 102.

91 Jimmy Carter, "Remarks by Former U.S. President at the Coretta Scott King Funeral," *Carter Center*, February 10 2006, http://www.cartercenter.org/news/documents/doc2295.html (January 29, 2007).

98 "Oprah Winfrey Pays Tribute to Coretta Scott King," *CNN.com*, (transcript of remarks, Atlanta, February 6, 2006). http://transcripts.cnn.com/TRANSCRIPTS/0602/06/lol.03.html (August 28, 2006).

98 Associated Press, "MPR: Remembering Coretta Scott King," *MPR*, January 31, 2006, http://news.minnesota.publicradio.org/features/2006/01/31_ap_corettaking (March 23, 2007).

98 Synthia Brown-Dyson, interview with author, August 23, 2006.

98 Dyer, Ervin, "Obituary: Coretta Scott King/ 'First Lady' of Civil Rights," *Pittsburgh Post-Gazette*, February 1, 2006, http://www.post-gazette.com/pg/06032/647676.stm (August 28, 2006).

99 Winfrey.

99 Ibid.

SELECTED BIBLIOGRAPHY

BOOKS

Branch, Taylor. *At Canaan's Edge: America in the King Years 1965–68*. New York: Simon & Schuster, 2006.

Branch, Taylor. *Parting the Waters: America in the King Years 1954–63*. New York: Simon & Schuster, 1988.

Branch, Taylor. *Pillar of Fire: America in the King Years 1963–65*. New York: Simon & Schuster, 1998.

Frady, Marshall. *Martin Luther King Jr.: A Life*. New York: Penguin Books, 2002.

Garrow, David J. *Bearing the Cross: Martin Luther King, Jr. and the Southern Christian Leadership Conference*. New York: Perennial Classics, 2004. Originally published in 1986.

King, Coretta Scott. *My Life with Martin Luther King Jr*. New York: Avon Books, 1979. Original copyright 1969.

King, Dexter Scott with Ralph Wiley. *Growing Up King: An Intimate Memoir*. New York: Warner Books, 2003.

King, Martin Luther, Jr. Edited by Clayborne Carson. *The Autobiography of Martin Luther King, Jr*. New York, Boston: IPM in association with Warner Books, 1988.

Thernstrom, Stephan and Abigail Thernstrom. *American in Black and White: One Nation, Indivisible*. New York: Simon & Schuster, 1997.

Vivian, Octavia. *Coretta: The Story of Coretta Scott King*. Commemorative Edition. Minneapolis: Fortress Press, 2006.

Williams, Juan. *Eyes on the Prize: America's Civil Rights Years, 1954–1965*. New York: Penguin Books, 1988. This edition published 2002.

ARTICLES

Academy of Achievement, Interview of Coretta Scott King, June 12, 2004. "First Lady of Civil Rights." Interspersed with remarks from Mrs. King's address to the Academy of Achievement at the National Cathedral in Washington, D.C. on June 18, 1999.

http://www.achievement.org/autodoc/page/kin1int-1 (March 26, 2007).

Applebome, Peter. "Coretta Scott King, A Civil Rights Icon, Dies at 78," *New York Times*. February 1, 2006. http://www.nytimes.com/2006/02/01/national/01king.html?ex=1 29645000&en=690e1ce8f5e0cb56&ei=5090 (March 26, 2007).

Bland, Cicely, interviewer. "King Kids Remember Mama," AtlantaTribune.com. n.d. http://www.atlantatribune.com/coretta.html (March 26, 2007).

"Celebrating Her Spirit: Coretta Scott King. April 27, 1927– January 30, 2006." Funeral Program.

Dyer, Ervin. "Obituary: Coretta Scott King 'First Lady' of civil rights," *Pittsburgh Post-Gazette*, Wednesday February 1, 2006. post-gazette.com. http://www.post-gazette.com/pg/ 06032/647676.stm (March 26, 2007).

King, Coretta Scott, Address at Antioch Reunion 2004, Antioch College. http://www.antioch-college.edu/news/csk/ 2004Mannacceptance.html (March 26, 2007).

King, Coretta Scott. "The Meaning of the Martin Luther King, Jr. Holiday." The King Center. http://www.thekingcenter.org/holiday/index.asp (March 26, 2007).

Norment, Lynn. "Coretta Scott King; The Woman Behind the King Anniversary." *Ebony*. January 1990, vol. 45, no 3.

Schmemann, Serge. "Coretta King Sees Apartheid Foe." *NYTimes.com*. September 12, 1986. http://www.nytimes.com/ (April 16, 2007).

Young, Andrew. "The Untold Story of Martin Luther King Jr. & Coretta Scott King." *Ebony*, April 2006.

INTERVIEWS

Author interview with Sister Cora Marie Billings, director, Office for Black Catholics, Diocese of Richmond, April 5, 2006.

Author interview with Synthia Brown-Dyson, bodyguard and close friend of Coretta Scott King, August 23, 2006.

FURTHER READING AND WEBSITES

BOOKS

Finlayson, Reggie. *Nelson Mandela*. Minneapolis: Twenty-First Century Books, 1999.

———. *We Shall Overcome: The History of the American Civil Rights Movement*. Minneapolis: Twenty-First Century Books, 2003.

Freedman, Russell. *Freedom Walkers: The Story of the Montgomery Bus Boycott*. New York: Holiday House. 2006.

Manheimer, Ann. *Martin Luther King Jr.: Dreaming of Equality*. Minneapolis: Twenty-First Century Books, 2005.

Martin, Christopher. *Mohandas Gandhi*. Minneapolis: Twenty-First Century Books, 2001.

Meltzer, Milton. *There Comes a Time: The Struggle for Civil Rights*. New York: Random House, 2001.

Morrison, Toni. *Remember: The Journey to School Integration*. Boston: Houghton Mifflin, 2004.

Pastan, Amy. *Martin Luther King, Jr.: A Photographic Story of a Life*. New York: DK Publishing Inc., 2004.

WEBSITES

Civil Rights Timeline by Borgna Brunner and Elisa Hanney
http://www.infoplease.com/spot/civilrightstimeline1.html. This site outlines the major events of the civil rights movement from 1954 through 2005.

Coretta Scott King Interview
http://www.achievement.org/autodoc/page/kin1int-1. This website features an interview with Mrs. King, a profile, a short biography, and a photo gallery.

The King Center
http://www.thekingcenter.org/csk/bio.html. This site contains a short biography as well as information on The King Center, Martin Luther King Jr., and the national holiday celebrating Dr. King.

INDEX

OTHER TITLES FROM LERNER AND BIOGRAPHY®:

Ariel Sharon
Arnold Schwarzenegger
Benito Mussolini
Benjamin Franklin
Bill Gates
Billy Graham
Carl Sagan
Che Guevara
Chief Crazy Horse
Colin Powell
Coretta Scott King
Daring Pirate Women
Edgar Allan Poe
Eleanor Roosevelt
Fidel Castro
Frank Gehry
George Lucas
George W. Bush
Gloria Estefan
Gwen Stefani
Hillary Rodham Clinton
Jack Kerouac
Jacques Cousteau
Jane Austen
J.K. Rowling
Joseph Stalin
Latin Sensations
Legends of Dracula
Legends of Santa Claus
Malcolm X

Mao Zedong
Mark Twain
Martha Stewart
Maya Angelou
Napoleon Bonaparte
Nelson Mandela
Osama bin Laden
Pope Benedict XVI
Pope John Paul II
Queen Cleopatra
Queen Elizabeth I
Queen Latifah
Rosie O'Donnell
Russell Simmons
Saddam Hussein
Shakira
Stephen Hawking
The Beatles
Thurgood Marshall
Tiger Woods
Tony Blair
V.I. Lenin
Vera Wang
Vladimir Putin
Wilma Rudolph
Winston Churchill
Women in Space
Women of the Wild West
Yasser Arafat

ABOUT THE AUTHOR

Stephanie Sammartino McPherson enjoys writing biographies for young people. She and her husband, Richard, live in Virginia but also call California home.

PHOTO ACKNOWLEDGMENTS

The images in this book are used with the permission of: © Michael Ochs Archives/Stringer/Getty Images, p. 2; National Archives, pp. 6, 91; © Dorothea Lang/Stringer/Time & Life Pictures/Getty Images, p. 10; © Gordon Parks/Time Life Pictures/Getty Images, p. 12; © The Everett Collection, p. 18; © Michael Ochs Archives/CORBIS, p. 23; © CORBIS, p. 27; © AFP/Stringer/Getty Images, p. 30; © AP Photo/Gene Herrick, pp. 33, 35, 40; © Don Cravens/Time & Life Pictures/Getty Images, p. 45; © Donald Uhrbrock/Time & Life Pictures/Getty Images, pp. 50, 54; The John F. Kennedy Library, [ST-C237-1-63], p. 57; © Bettmann/CORBIS, pp. 58, 74; © Time & Life Pictures/Stringer/Getty Images, p. 60; © Hulton-Deutsch Collection/CORBIS, p. 63; © Flip Schulke/CORBIS, p. 68; The Lyndon B. Johnson Presidential Library, p. 70; © Vernon Merritt III/Time & Life Pictures/Getty Images, p. 78; © Art Shay/Time & Life and Pictures/Getty Images, p. 82; © Hulton Archive/Getty Images, p. 84; © KPA/ZUMA Press, p. 88; © Luke Frazza/AFP/Getty Images, p. 95; © Allison Silberberg/Getty Images, pp. 97, 98; © AP Photo/W. A. Harewood, p. 101

Front cover: © Robin Nelson/ZUMA Press.
Back cover: Courtesy of Antioch College